# From Teacher

# to

# Instructional Designer

## Practical Steps to Start
## Your New Career

Erika L. Martin, M.Ed., MBA

To every educator seeking a new career, a new life-- this is for you!

# Table of Contents

# Introduction: My Teacher Transition Journey

In the early part of my career while working in international business I noticed a backlog in various processes from time to time. This slowed my work down and others around me. So, I began to look for gaps in performance in collaboration with managers. Together we developed training to fill those gaps. During this process I was taking surveys and meeting with subject matter experts (SMEs) to analyze skills gaps and to create training to improve the skills of professionals. I loved creating facilitators and participant guides, and leading training for years. After some time, though, I felt that I could make a greater contribution to my community by collaborating with younger learners. Which led to my career in education where I have spent almost two decades teaching children, and training educators and district leaders as a consultant (for the past eight years).

When the pandemic hit in 2020, I was trying my best to reach 1st graders through the computer screen during reading as they giggled and walked around the room. My colleagues and I all dedicated longer hours to ensure all standards in math and English were being met and taught. What we did not expect, however, was a lack of enthusiasm for virtual learning. I asked myself if I really wanted more of this. I collaborated tirelessly with English Learners for years, loving every minute of it. But this? Marry that experience with the more recent dominance in education of too many voices-- many without wisdom or knowledge that dictate what goes on in the classroom, or what does not (thereby omitting what should).

Fast forward to 2021 and my search for a new career. I immediately investigated Instructional Design. What I found was a community of adult learners who found a new energy while studying instructional design. My first thoughts were: I design instruction! I wonder if my teaching skills and experience would fit into this role. Then, I began reading dozens of educators' posts on LinkedIn who were studying or had already begun working as

1

instructional designers, or IDs. They all had one thing in common—*they were happy!* So, I began my online studies and have enjoyed it ever since.

What I learned immediately is that Learning and Development (L&D) has changed greatly since I started working in business. I also discovered that training design requires following learning theory, stringent guidelines, and industry standards. In short, I quickly realized that I needed to go back to school to become an instructional designer.

As you investigate instructional design as a career, you will discover that many of your teaching skills correlate to those of an instructional designer. Your experience in writing curriculum, managing data-driven learning experiences (lessons and assessments), creating anchor charts, or infographics as well as managing educational programs relate to this new role. (More in Chapter 2). For now, just know that if you are considering a career in Instructional Design and you are an educator, you might very well find your niche here. What instructional designers do that teachers mimic is create learning experiences based on data so that professionals can learn more skills or knowledge. There are many facets to the role of an ID and *much of the work you have done until now as an educator is directly relatable.*

It is the beginning of 2023, and I am thrilled to put this book together for the many teachers who asked me about instructional design. I hope by publishing this book, I can offer you the answers to your questions in a more succinct and efficient manner. This book is meant to be a practical guide to the Instructional Design profession, specifically how to get there. Here I hope to offer greater clarity into what the ID role is, necessary training, and top technologies used today. I also cover the time and financial investment required to pursue this profession. You will also find tips on writing your ID resume, how to network and other effective job-hunting skills I developed during my corporate career.

The information here is based on my experience and knowledge and is not meant to be exhaustive. As you research this profession you will find many resources and industry experts. At the end of the book in the Resources section, you will find a list of websites and books that can enhance your training as an Instructional Designer. Make sure to take advantage of various resources throughout your journey so that you can become a well-rounded ID.

It is also my great hope that you will undertake the soul searching many of us have done while changing careers. By doing so, you will be better prepared to move into a new work life that offers creativity, writing, and design. (Not to mention peace of mind!) To help facilitate this process, I include Chapter 8 which offers the opportunity to answer reflective questions, sparking your thinking as you make decisions for your future.

To my fellow educators who are thinking about transitioning into Instructional Design-- you can do this! Remember, you have the intelligence, skills, and experience to soar!


Erika L. Martin

# Chapter 1  The Instructional Designer Role –
## The Basics

For you to enter this new career field of instructional design it is important to get an idea of what the instructional design job is first. So, in this chapter I give you a snapshot of the role. You will gain a broader perspective of the profession and all it entails once you are in training. My goal for you here is to offer a basic overview of the job itself.

> Instructional Design is the process of systematic design and development of effective, efficient, and engaging learning experiences.

> Instructional Designers create effective and efficient (and engaging) learning experiences. They create training modules online and in person as well as learning materials.

The work of an instructional designer (ID) is many faceted, like that of an educator. However, instructional designers focus their skills on training adult learners. As the educator looks for gaps in knowledge and skills, so does the instructional designer. However, the instructional designer analyzes larger scopes of problems in industry. Gaps can occur in many aspects of work, processes, tasks, skills and more. If gaps are discovered in knowledge or skills, then and only then is training designed to fill these gaps. Thereafter, the instructional designer develops training modules, implements training, and analyzes the effectiveness of that training. This role demands collaborating well with Subject Matter Experts (SMEs), managers, leaders, marketing, and sales professionals, accountants as well as technology experts (all stakeholders) in an organization.

Furthermore, instructional designers must be excellent communicators and project managers. Yes, project managers. As an ID, you will collaborate in discussions to determine all stakeholders' needs and compile documentation. You may manage training design projects and maintain deliverable schedules for development. Once training is decided upon as the right path to take, you write an outline of the course that establishes the learning goals and learner expectations. In addition to the outline, the instructional designer writes the Storyboard. The Storyboard is the *Bible* of the course, with all the design items, graphics, visuals, text, and notes. It is also the guiding element within the design process as it is approved by management (and all stakeholders) to ensure that the most effective training will be designed. Once it's approved, the Storyboard becomes the basis for all that will be included in the course. In addition, instructional designers carry numerous responsibilities throughout the entire project—analysis, design, development, implementation, and evaluation. You will gain a better understanding of the ID's role further on in this chapter when you read about the ADDIE project framework.

Currently, training occurs through various methods. One can rollout training through the ILT process, or Instructor-Led Training where a facilitator leads adult learners in a classroom environment. (VILT is virtual ILT.) A blended learning experience or training combines aspects of ILT and eLearning. eLearning involves developing online or web-based training. It is highly popular as there are several advantages to using eLearning courses to train employees. For one, adult learners can access their courses online and study at their own pace on convenient iPhones and tablets. Two, eLearning courses and learner data are easily hosted on a company's LMS (Learning Management System) where scores are maintained, and the results discussed with managers. Three, many eLearning courses now include Gamification, the latest technology that makes learning highly engaging. Gamification is one of the latest components in eLearning course design and development. When incorporated into eLearning platforms, gamification utilizes elements of games (points, leveling, competition, etc.) to train and motivate adult learners in real life situations. For the instructional designer, this involves adding a game layer to a real-life training module.

Becoming an instructional designer means studying many learning theories. A vital part of designing training involves understanding Adult Learning Theory (Malcolm Knowles). Adult Learning Theory is an integral part and underlying basis for training design and development, i.e., how adults learn. There are six assumptions as part of adult motivation with regards to learning.

- Adults must be in control of their learning.
- Adults must have topics that relate directly to their work.
- Adults use problem-solving in real-life situations in their learning process.
- Adults relate their life experiences to help them learn.
- Adults are highly intrinsically motivated learners (earn a living, etc.).

- Adults need to know the reason for learning.

As part of building your knowledge in the foundations of instructional design you will also learn about various project management frameworks. These frameworks shape the process of how training develops. Thus, knowing various frameworks is vital for your success as an instructional designer. (Different organizations use different frameworks.) These include ADDIE, SAM (Successive Approximation Model), Action Mapping, Dick & Carey's Systems Approach Model, and more. Major frameworks include analyzing a problem, finding a solution, designing the solution, and developing that solution. For our purposes, I introduce the ADDIE framework to help you gain a basic understanding of the instructional designer's role.

ADDIE stands for Analysis, Design, Development, Implementation and Evaluation. The ADDIE framework is non-linear and has five phases with Evaluation interwoven throughout the entire process. The Analysis phase involves the process of discovery, looking for gaps in knowledge, processes, and skills. This phase includes many tasks, including performing a Needs Analysis. In general, during the Needs Analysis the ID asks focused questions to managers, employees, and SMEs about the context, the learners, and the tasks. Within the Context Analysis IDs look to answer why there is a gap between employee performance and the organization's goals: why learners are not performing as expected and what learners need to do after training. The Learner Analysis answers questions regarding what the learners already know and what they need to know to do their jobs. This includes how adept learners are at the technologies used on the job, demographics, and a survey to make sure training is learner-centered. The Task Analysis covers which tasks learners need to do efficiently within a standard set of procedures. Throughout the Needs Analysis, instructional designers complete surveys, questionnaires, interviews, and observations using focus groups and collaborate with SMEs and other stakeholders. After all the data is collected, the analysis of this information determines if training is needed. If training is decided upon then the appropriate training is designed. There are many types of Needs Analyses, three major ones are: Knowledge & Skills Assessment, Job & Task Analysis, and Competency-based Needs Assessment.

The Design phase is where IDs begin to design the training. They write learning objectives in the course Outline, obtain vital information from Subject Matter Experts (SMEs), compose content and eventually the Storyboard itself. The Storyboard houses all the design elements and the entire course, including brand colors, graphics, videos, fonts, all the text--all the content as it will be presented to the learners.

In the next stage, Development, the course and all the associated assets are created according to the type of training (ILT, blended, eLearning). By the end of this phase the course is developed to completion and is ready to be rolled out. Here is where courses are developed as well as all learning materials like facilitator and participant guides and job aids.

During Implementation, the course is rolled out or delivered to learners. Careful consideration goes into this process to make sure there are sufficient computers, space and so on. Delivering training can take place via a Learning Management System (LMS), within physical office space or through electronic means like an email server. If one is delivering training through an ILT course, there is a dry run of the training, and attendees are notified of dates and times.

In the Evaluation stage one measures the effectiveness of the course by analyzing performance and learning data. Depending on the organization, various internal metrics are used to measure the Return on Investment (ROI). (A training course really has no value until it adds value to the organization and its learners.) Training is reevaluated and revised to improve its effectiveness. The instructional designer participates in all five phases of the project. However, depending upon the organization and the scope of the project, an ID may work in specific phases or on specific tasks.

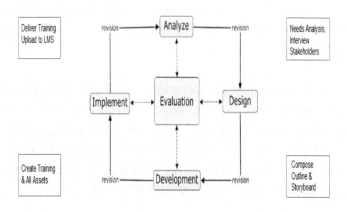

To give you an idea of some of the ID's responsibilities within each phase of the ADDIE framework, I include Figure 1.1.

Figure 1.1 ADDIE a non-linear framework

Working as an instructional designer offers great flexibility. There are three professional paths you can choose from: employee, contractor, or freelancer. It is helpful to understand these three paths to better discern which role is best suited for you. There are instructional designers who choose to become regularly employed staff members within organizations to get on-the-job experience and grow professionally that way. Others choose to become independent and freelance. Then, there are those who want greater choice and control over the projects they work on and become contractors. Whichever one you choose, make sure it fits your needs and your work style.

Employee – Instructional designers are hired into organizations directly and receive all the benefits as an employee. This includes health insurance and retirement plans, where offered. The nature of the ID job differs depending on the organization of the company. Some IDs work on large teams while others work independently. Make sure you determine this when you interview. If you want to work in a team and there is none to be found keep looking.

Contractor- As a contractor, you will work for a recruiting agency that offers you a contract. This contract is a legally binding agreement allowing you to work on a specific project and for a specific amount of time. Contracts can run for several weeks up to many months. One advantage to this type of work is having the freedom to choose different projects over time and develop knowledge in various industries and business areas. As a contractor, you may be offered health insurance after the first 30-60 days. The recruiting agency takes care of the hiring process and all the paperwork it entails. Another great advantage is the possibility to become a regular employee depending on employment opportunities.

Freelancer – As a freelancing instructional designer, you will be a business owner. You will need to register your business, usually as an LLC or Limited Liability company. If you register as a small business as a minority, you are eligible to bid on government contracts. You can register your business online or hire an attorney to do this for you. Once your business is officially up and running, the Freelance ID establishes contacts and uses their network to attain contracts for work. Freelancing has the advantage of working for yourself and setting your own schedule. However, it demands you find projects on your own. Having a network and good contacts is essential to be a successful Freelancer. LinkedIn is a major source to find freelancing jobs (see Chapter 7). As a Freelancer, you will need to provide your own health insurance and pay for all your own business costs (computer, software, office supplies, etc.).

Whichever career path you follow, I encourage you to seek out colleagues and connect with those who have direct experience working in these distinct roles. That way, you will have a better picture of the advantages and disadvantages of each.

# Chapter 2 Your Valuable and Transferrable Teaching Skills

With regards to educators, one thing is certain—they have the experience, training and skills that give them a major advantage over others who enter this career. Educators have studied learning theory, developed differentiated curricula and assessments, managed student data on learning management systems (LMS), used data-driven instruction and assessment, to name just a few professional experiences that create a superior skills base.

Table 2.1 shows a list of educators' transferable skills juxtaposed with those of instructional designers. Please note that the jargon under the Educator column translates into the business verbiage used in instructional design. While there are many skills that correlate between both professionals, I chose to highlight 10 of the major skills educators possess. While your teaching skills relate to those of an instructional designer, keep in mind that training is necessary to fully transition into those skills. As you review the chart you may want to reflect on all the work you have done in your teaching role. Making a list of all your accomplishments should astound you! (More in Chapter 6.)

Table 2.1 Transferrable Educator Skills

| EDUCATOR | INSTRUCTIONAL DESIGNER |
|---|---|
| Curriculum Writer | Authors: Outlines, Storyboards, Design Documents, & more |
| Differentiated Instruction and Assessment | Customized Learning Experiences and Quizzing |
| Learning Theory (Pedagogy) | Adult Learning Theory (Andragogy) |
| Data-driven Instruction MTSS, RTI (U.S. Intervention programs) | Results-driven Coursework: Knowledge Checks & Assessments |
| Student Data Management, Blackboard, School-based LMS | Learning Management System LMS |
| Co-Teaching, Professional Learning Community (PLCs) | Project Collaborator/Leader |
| Bloom's Taxonomy, Curriculum & Lesson Design | Standard for Learning Objectives & Learner Expectations |
| Anchor charts & worksheets | Infographics design & worksheets |
| Web-based Instruction | eLearning Course Development |
| Education Program Management | Project Management |
| Teacher | Training Facilitator |

After looking at the information in Table 2.1, what is your initial response? Are you surprised? How does this make you feel as you consider entering this new career? If anything, I hope you feel empowered! Educators possess the expertise of transforming learning standards with skills and knowledge gaps to create differentiated ("customized") learning experiences in a way that no other professional can! Educators come *more* prepared into the instructional design career than any other professional. Please keep this in mind as you explore this career.

As stated, earlier educators have many skills, and they include:

- Project Management
- Excellent Time Management
- Deadline-Oriented
- Leadership
- Training Facilitation Expertise
- Blended-Learning & ILT Experts (Instructor-led training)
- Flexible
- Creative
- Resilient
- Resourceful
- Collaborators
- and more!

After reviewing all this information, I hope you are feeling confident about your ability to start on your path to instructional design. One thing I suggest here is to take time and write down the skills you have. You will work on a similar task in Chapter 6. For now, though, I want you to just think about all the many aspects of teaching, including all your duties. Perhaps begin with your morning routine and all that it entails. Then, look at all the writing you do, your collaboration on grade teams and school-based teams, leadership teams, etc. Do not overlook record keeping and assessment writing. If you are a coach, map out your day to reflect on how many teachers you meet with, how you are helping them develop their skills, look at the data collection and analysis process as well. The more you know yourself, the greater ability you will have to express this knowledge and be better able to transfer your many skills into this new career.

One of the most exciting times on your path to becoming an instructional designer is when your training begins. You will quickly see how your valuable experience in education enables you to grasp theoretical concepts and apply these to the design process. For example, during training I was working on the design phase to complete the writing of an eLearning course Outline. While I was writing, the trainer mentioned Bloom's Taxonomy and the essential content used to compose learning goals. My only reaction was excitement and a huge boost of confidence. Learning innovative technologies can be challenging. Studying instructional design demands practice and revising projects and assets. If in the middle of all this work you can find a word, a concept or a task that matches your experience and skills, it gives you that boost necessary to succeed. Take it from me, I latched onto every aspect of the process that hit home, sat well with me, and became the basis of my encouragement. So, be encouraged, the same will happen to you! Grasp onto everything that magnifies your prior knowledge and skills. This will give you greater confidence as you study and design.

# Chapter 3   Training You Need & Where to Find It

As you embark on becoming skilled as an instructional designer, you will discover that there are many training options available to you. There are free courses, fee-based, in-person and online courses, to name a few. As many of you have remarkably busy lives and may still be teaching, it is common for educators to choose an online training course to get started. I opted into this for myself and found it most convenient. In this Chapter, I provide lists of degree programs, training programs, and courses. As with any new training, I encourage you to do an internet search, consult with your colleagues and with teachers already working in the field to gather as much information as possible. This will equip you to make the most informed choices and decisions as to which programs of study will meet your unique needs in terms of your time and financial commitments.

Furthermore, I highly recommend that you connect with educators through LinkedIn (and other networks mentioned here) who are working as instructional designers and who have made the transition already. These professionals have firsthand experience and knowledge about the role, training, and various industries where they work. To do so, you will need a LinkedIn account and an active profile. (See Chapter 7.)

Whether you decide to begin instructional design training part- or full-time, one of the most important things to remember is that it is a commitment—both a time and financial investment. I chose a training program because I wanted to be in a cohort, have a portfolio by the end of the coursework and build a network with alumni. When I began the coursework, I made the commitment to study seven to eight hours a day. I continue to learn, as an instructional designer never stops learning. Maintaining a growth mindset is an essential element to one's success.

Training organizations and universities create programs to meet the needs of adult learners and their different schedules. So, there are training programs that are eight weeks, nine months all the way up to two years. You can study instructional design course-by-course, or dive into a whole program of study, as I did. I found it to be extremely beneficial to enter a whole program for several reasons. For one, there are mentors and coaches who offer professional advice and help you become better at design (visual, eLearning and more). Two, peer feedback is a major part of the learning process. If you find a training program that includes this, you will have the advantage of going through various iterations of your designs with much support. Three, many of these programs offer the cohort-based learning model--the gold standard used in training today. (A cohort is a cohesive group of learners who experience learning together.) Fourth, a program of study offers an organized learning plan. There are many aspects to instructional design so good organization is vital. You will also have access to videos, webinars, and additional support in a program. Effective programs will have the components described in Diagram 3.1.

# Diagram 3.1 Essential Components of ID Training Programs

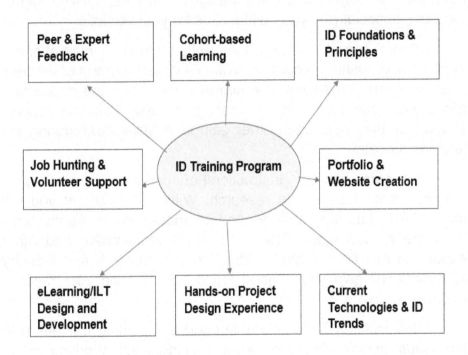

| Peer & Expert Feedback | Cohort-based Learning | ID Foundations & Principles |

**ID Training Program**

Job Hunting & Volunteer Support

Portfolio & Website Creation

eLearning/ILT Design and Development

Hands-on Project Design Experience

Current Technologies & ID Trends

[Design: EL Martin]

Here are components to look for in an ID program as you begin your search for training and furthering your education. Peer feedback is a powerful component in the training process. When one receives feedback, one has the advantage of gaining valuable insight from others. Others analyze your designs and discuss them with you. In this process you will offer your own comments/advice to others as well. Mentors and coaches who are industry experts have the final say in approving designs. Their expertise is highly valuable, especially as you build assets for your portfolio.

Cohort-based Learning is currently on the rise internationally in all kinds of training programs. Within a cohort a group of learners study the same materials at a similar pace. This kind of learning elicits more cohesion and the sharing of ideas. Learners receive support as they help each other gain innovative ideas during the learning process.

Research-based Instruction/Foundations is providing learning content based on research. Within this content you will study Adult Learning theory, project management frameworks, color theory and more. There are many researchers and other experts in this field of study. Studying the research and industry standards will give you a good foundation to build your designs upon.

Job Hunting & Volunteer Support is providing trainees with job leads and/or Volunteer work opportunities. Working for a volunteer client is highly advantageous as it allows you to gain experience, hone design skills and build relationships that can lead to employment. Having volunteer design experience on your resume can only strengthen it.

Portfolio creation is vital. During training you will need to make a portfolio of your best work. Industry experts will help you do this within a training program. In fact, effective programs have this as central to completing their program. I cannot stress this enough—you *need* a portfolio to make it to the interview.

Designing and developing eLearning and ILT are essential skills for instructional designers. Look for programs that cover industry-standard eLearning technologies, color theory, graphic and visual design basics as well as technologies for creating all assets.

Hands-on Project Design Experience is exactly what it says, you create projects as you study. This involves using technology for eLearning, video making, graphic design and more. The main point here is to gain ongoing practice so that design skills can be learned and improved.

Latest Technologies and ID Trends are covered in an effective training program. Your goal as an ID is to have a good number of technologies under your belt so that you can be hired to do the technical work that is demanded and expected. Gamification is on the rise, so finding training in this technology is highly advantageous.

During your training you will also rediscover Bloom's Taxonomy. Bloom's Taxonomy is a standard component in developing training courses. Instructional designers base their learning objectives on the verbiage from Bloom's framework with focus on the top three skills of his learning theory pyramid: Analyze, Evaluate and Create. As an ID, you will be using Bloom's Taxonomy verbiage to compose learning objectives and learning expectations for adult learners. (As you can see, there are areas in instructional design where you will find direct correlation to your experience as an educator.)

It should be clear to you by now that additional training *is essential* to becoming an instructional designer. Please breathe here! Getting the skills and knowledge you need *is doable.* There are many educators who have acquired the skills they needed and have made the transition into this career within a reasonable amount of time. How? They learned new skills and knowledge by building upon their foundation—their training and experience as educators.

There is another component to training that is important. If you are going to choose a program that is educational and U.S. based, you want to make sure it has been accredited by a state or local Education Authority. This is particularly applicable to university programs. This is to ensure that certifications earned are authentic and validated by an official source. There are programs that offer several types of certificates. Make sure that these certifications are valid and earn you the professional credentials and titles towards which you are working. Otherwise, you may be wasting precious time. Instructional Design *is a profession* and as such you want to ensure that you will earn credentials that represent the skills you master throughout your studies. Universities offer professional certificates, and one pays a higher fee for those. You can easily pay over $5000 for a short program and over $25,000 for a master's degree.

Finally, when you are choosing your program make sure it meets your individual needs. Do the research, it will save you time in the end. This is an investment in your future, so choose your coursework and program wisely.

<u>Training Programs & Courses</u>

In this section I provide a list of degree and non-degree instructional design programs to get you acquainted with them. Some of the organizations included here are ones I have direct experience with, or ones my colleagues have recommended to me. The experts and their programs listed under non-degree programs all come highly recommended by program participants based on reviews. In no way do I recommend any program over the over; nor is this list exclusive. There are hundreds of programs and courses to choose from. Again, choosing training that furthers your education is a major decision that you must make for yourself based on your unique needs and goals.

One of the best ways to get your feet wet is to take some free courses where you gain insight into the field of instructional design. Some career changers take courses for a couple of months, some decide on a more formal route and enroll in an ID training program or university degree program. You do not need a master's degree to work as an instructional designer. However, you do need solid training that will give you the foundations and principles of instructional design and current technologies, especially for eLearning. This takes time. University certificate programs are typically several months long, and master's degrees can take one and a half to two years to complete. Furthermore, most non-degree training programs often called "Bootcamps" or "Academies" run anywhere from two months to one year. Some of these programs offer lifetime access to the coursework, which is extremely helpful in reviewing the learning material and practicing technical skills. The most important thing to remember is that what you put into a program is what you will get out of it. I studied seven to eight hours a day for months because I had the time and wanted to get the most out of my program. Becoming an instructional designer requires study and practice. The more time you give yourself to do this, the higher skilled you will become. If you decide on a cohort-based learning program, be prepared to share your work and feedback on a regular basis. This is a vital part of the whole learning process.

Program and course content and pricing are apt to change at any time. To get the most up-to-date information it is best to contact the program coordinators directly. Again, I encourage you to expand this list on your own. Use this list as a springboard. This way you can make the most informed decision for furthering your education. So, start researching and look beyond the organizations and experts I provide here. I want you to be able to choose the best program of study that meets your needs, both in terms of time and financial investment.

Furthermore, please be aware that additional costs can arise during training programs where participants may need to or opt in to purchasing software licenses. This is particularly helpful when maintaining created asset files, especially those added to personal website portfolios. You will want to learn more about any additional costs *before* you begin studying, especially within a fee-based program of study. Also, keep in mind that acquiring further education does not guarantee employment. Your devotion to your goals and perseverance will help you succeed.

<u>Degree Programs & Certificates</u>

Universities offer online professional certificate programs and master's degrees. Certificate programs start at $5,000 and degrees at $25,000 (tuition based on in/out-of-state rates). Here is a list of recent universities ranked in the top 10 of the U.S. News & World Report for Online Master's in Educational/Instructional Media Design Programs*.

*Arizona State University- Graduate Certificate (15 hrs.) in Instructional Design and Performance Improvement. Instructional Design and Performance Improvement (Graduate Certificate) - Certificate | Degree Details | ASU Degree Search Learning Design and Technologies M.Ed. degree (30 credits). Learning Design and Technologies, MEd - MED | Degree Details | ASU Degree Search

*Indiana University Bloomington – Master of Science, Instructional Systems Technology (36 credits). Instructional Systems Technology (M.S.Ed.) - School of Education: Degrees & Majors: Academics: Indiana University Bloomington

*Pennsylvania State University World Campus – Master's in Education Learning, Design and Technology (30 credits). https://www.worldcampus.psu.edu/degrees-and-certificates/penn-state-online-masters-in-learning-design-technology/overview

Certificate: 12 credit Certificate in E-Learning Design https://www.worldcampus.psu.edu/degrees-and-certificates/penn-state-online-e-learning-design-certificate/overview

Purdue University Learning Design and Technology Program – Several Master's programs to choose from. https://online.purdue.edu/programs/education/masters-in-education-learning-design-technology

*University of Florida- Certificate (12 credits) in Instructional Design. https://education.ufl.edu/educational-technology/online-certificates/instructional-design/

## Degree Programs & Certificates

*University of Georgia- Online Master's degree in Learning, Design & Technology, Instructional Design and Development (36 credits). https://online.uga.edu/degrees-certificates/med-learning-design-technology-instructional-design-development

There is also a Certificate program: Introduction to Instructional Design and Practicum (3 credits each). https://www.georgiacenter.uga.edu/courses/teaching-and-education/instructional-design-and-elearning-certificate

University of West Florida- The Master's degree includes certificates. https://onlinedegrees.uwf.edu/online-degrees/med-masters-instructional-design-performance-technology/

## Non-Degree Training Programs & Courses

Pricing varies on all fee-based courses and programs, so check the websites.

**Adobe** – Adobe offers free tutorials and user guides for their software programs, including the Captivate User Community. www.adobe.com

**Articulate 360** – There are free tutorials and webinars for Rise and Storyline on the website through Articulate 360 Training as well as a learning community. www.articulate.com

**ATD** – Association for Talent Development is the national association for Learning and Development. The Association offers membership, national chapter networking events and more. Choose from over 170 courses, including a Virtual Instructional Design course. Professional certifications offered. www.td.org

**Coursera** – Numerous online courses ranging from several weeks to months. Course fees vary. Courses offered through universities. Certificates offered. www.coursera.org

**Devlin Peck** – Industry-celebrated ID/entrepreneur. He offers free videos on multiple topics related to ID through YouTube and a fee-based Bootcamp. www.devlinpeck.com

**Eduflow Academy** – Free online courses and programs, as well as fee-based courses. Coursework varies in topic and length throughout the year and includes topics like Instructional Design Principles for Course Creation. Certificates offered. www.eduflow.com/academy

**THE ELEARNING DESIGNER'S ACADEMY** – Tim Slade, industry-celebrated ID expert and author. He offers an 8-week course that includes his eLearning book, a learning community, coaching, hands-on eLearning design, building a portfolio, lifetime access to the course and more. https://elearningacademy.io/academy/

**Jeff Batt**- technology guru offers online training courses through Udemy and Pluralsight. He is an expert at Articulate Storyline 360 and other technologies like Java Script and HTML5. www.pluralsight.com and www.udemy.com To find his courses, enter his name under Search.

**Learning Strategy and Design**-Jill Davidian, veteran ID offers two free introductory courses, the ID Jumpstart, and the ID Launchpad. The fee-based 9-month Academy (AIDA) is a self-paced, step-by-step course with continuous coaching. Rise 360 and VYOND included. www.learningstrategyanddesign.com

**LinkedIn Learning** - Free online coursework offered at participating U.S. public libraries and first 30-day Premium membership. Full access offered through Premium membership, $39 per month for the basic plan. Certificates offered. Various courses range from eLearning technologies to learning theory. www.linkedinlearning.com

**Mastering Instructional Design** – Connie Malamed, award winning ID and author. Take the 8-week Instructional Design Master Class as part of membership in this learning community. Learn through live classes, on-demand courses, and a supportive community. On-demand courses include instructional design, visual design, accessibility, Storyline and more. www.masteringid.com

## Non-Degree Training Programs & Courses

**Ray Pastore, PhD**., ID veteran, offers free videos on various ID topics. Some of the topics include Needs Analysis, Figuring Out Your Hourly Rate, and more. Look for him on YouTube by entering his name under Search. www.YouTube.com

**Rued Riis** (VYOND) Animated video software expert. He offers many free videos on YouTube, and fee-based courses. The fee-based online explainer video creation workshop, Explain Academy, is 4 weeks long. You will find him on YouTube and on his website. https://www.ruedriis.com/store

**Udemy** – Numerous courses to choose from many topics including Instructional Design Courses. You will find Jeff Batt's courses here as well. www.udemy.com

**YouTube**- There are numerous experts and their courses found here. Many experts give courses through free videos with information on their fee-based training workshops and bootcamps. Type: "Instructional Design Course" or individual names of experts listed here in the Search box. www.youtube.com

# Chapter 4 Technologies that Put You at the Top

A major part of the instructional designer's job is to design and develop learning experiences and training with the use of many different technologies, especially with regards to eLearning. As you study to become an instructional designer you will find that each training program uses specific technologies. It is therefore common for a student to learn additional technologies needed in their job that is not included in their program. For example, one ID training program might base eLearning design using Articulate 360 while another uses Adobe software programs, like Captivate. Nevertheless, effective training programs will include the use of the most current and widely used technologies.

The cost of becoming an instructional designer is also determined by the type of training you choose and which (and how many) software licenses you decide to purchase. As I previously mentioned, it is common during a program of study to buy software programs. For example, ID training program coordinators might offer a 30-day free trial, but one needs this time to develop an eLearning course and post it to a website as part of the portfolio. For recruiters to see the course, the software program must be active. It can take over 30 days to create eLearning courses and other assets and certainly longer to get hired into a job. That is why it becomes necessary to purchase licenses. This is especially true if you plan to become a contractor or freelancer when you need to provide your own software licenses. Having said this, please be aware that many software companies do offer their own 30-day free trials to get your feet wet. The good news is that there are teacher discounts offered by some software companies, usually to those who are still actively teaching and can provide a district/school email address.

Whichever programs you do choose to purchase, make sure that they are industry current. You do not need to purchase a lot of software programs to do this job. However, you will need some basic programs to get started. Your ID program directors will guide you in this as you gain hands-on experience. To get started with eLearning design and development, one usually needs three to four basic software programs: eLearning, graphic design, video, and voice over programs. Furthermore, it is extremely helpful to have some software licenses so you can use them and practice designing at your leisure. I personally purchased several software programs at the beginning of my ID training program and am glad that I did. This enabled me to create assets for my portfolio and maintain them long-term on my website.

On the next page are four basic areas of technology generally required to begin the design and development of eLearning training courses. This is a good starting point for studying and gaining the necessary skills for eLearning course design and development.

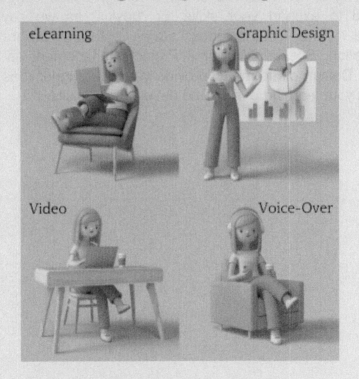

4 eLearning Design Components

eLearning

Graphic Design

Video

Voice-Over

To Get You Started

Design: EL Martin Images: Freepik.com

The following list includes popular technologies used today. You will use some of these in training and learn others as you expand your portfolio and design skills. If I failed to mention that becoming an ID requires ongoing learning, I say it now. As a designer it is vital to continue learning new knowledge, technologies, and skills. To find current prices on software licenses, I suggest doing an internet search for each company. Also, be aware that popular technologies can differ internationally. So, if you are looking to work abroad or for a foreign-based company, be prepared to expand your skills. or "upskill" as we say in the industry. The list includes savvy software programs for Gamification, Scenario Building, Project Management as well as Website Design platforms to provide you with suggestions as you broaden your learning design and development skills.

Technologies

**eLearning**

Articulate 360: Rise 360 & Storyline 360 (top-rated)

Adobe Captivate

**Graphic Design**

CANVA

Adobe Illustrator

**Video Making**

VYOND

Camtasia

Snagit

**Voice-Over (for Video)**

Audacity

Windows Voice Recorder

**Scenario Building**

Twine

Miro

<u>Technologies</u>

**Gamification**

Spinify

Genially

**Project Management Tools**

Asana

Trello

Wrike

**Website Design**

Google Sites

Weebly

Wix

WordPress

# Chapter 5 Assets that Get You Noticed

While expectations may vary depending on the employer or recruiter, there are basic assets, or things you design and create that will help you get the attention of hiring managers. One major advantage to getting interviews is to create an online portfolio. The portfolio is a collection of your best work, or assets you will have made during your studies (and that get approved by experts in the field, like mentors and coaches). You will have a great advantage over other candidates if you have your portfolio in hand and ready to share with employers. Below is a suggested list.

Portfolio Assets:

- eLearning Courses (2 or more, each in different eLearning software programs)
- Graphic Design assets (GIFs, logos, etc.)
- Job Aids
- Infographics
- Videos
- ILT assets: a slide deck (PowerPoint), facilitator, and participant guides
- A Website to host the portfolio (optional)
- Links to your resume and LinkedIn profile
- A link to Connect.

There are differing opinions about the minimum number of assets one should include in their portfolio. It is a clever idea to have at least two eLearning courses, a video, and several graphic design assets. A complete portfolio will highlight ILT assets as well. The more assets you have in your portfolio the greater your ability to show off your newly acquired design and development skills. A portfolio is non-negotiable. It is an industry standard so start creating one as soon as you can. You will thank yourself when you see the positive effect it has on your job hunt. Thankfully, many programs incorporate the portfolio as a mandatory component to completing one's training.

How do I get my portfolio out there, you might ask. Well, creating your own website to host the portfolio. I used Google Sites. The advantage to using Google is that you can house your documents (outlines, storyboards, etc.) in Google Docs and Google Slides and easily upload these into Sites. There are many other website platforms where you can create a great portfolio. The first three listed under Website Design in the technology list are free. Make sure to upload only your finest assets into your website— ones that show off your eLearning design/development skills, visual/graphic design abilities and more. Think of the portfolio as your technology resume!

With regards to having a website, I found that having designed and created my own helped a great deal in getting interviews. Right now, you may be thinking that creating a website is out of range for you or it is not necessary. Having a website will place you above the competition. As part of the interview process, Human Resource professionals asked me if I had website design skills, and it was gratifying to say Yes! Furthermore, I believe having a website to be the reason I made it to Round #2 interviews with hiring managers. It is obvious *that you are entering a technical job and as such you must be able to show off your technical skills* which reflect your value as a designer to employers. Do not sell yourself short! It is possible for recruiters to find you without a website, but if you make your best work available on the internet it will give you a tremendous advantage.

Here are five basic steps to take to become an instructional designer:

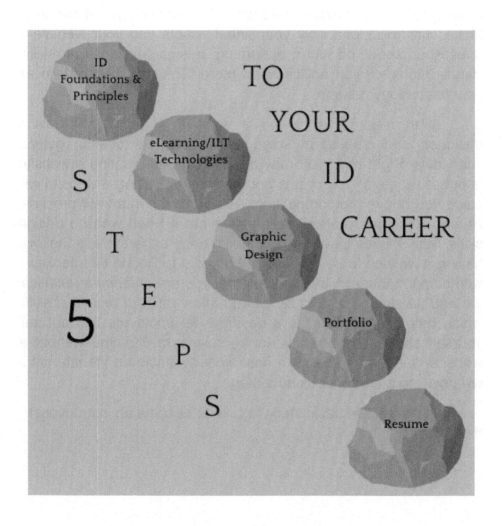

[Design: EL Martin\CANVA]

# Chapter 6 The ID Resume that Opens the Door

Your resume. A resume is a picture of your experiences and skills that must be composed in a way to set you apart from every other candidate. Each one of you is unique and each of you has exclusive experiences and skills. Here is where you highlight these! I have been composing resumes for years by aligning them to the most current trends in recruiting. I believe this has made all the difference in my own hiring success. Remember, a beautifully written resume will do the work *for* you—show your awesomeness and open doors!

In this chapter I cover each bullet point and include a resume template at the end so that you can get started writing your own. Resume writing is a skill but if you follow my tips here you will be able to begin composing a great one. The sooner you begin writing your resume, the better prepared you will be to start applying for jobs. I recommend you begin applying for work as soon as you have that stellar resume.

Starting to write a resume can feel like a daunting task, but if you break it down into parts it will become manageable. By the end of this chapter, you will have the information you need to compose one that is well-written. Here is a list of necessary components:

<u>Basic Resume Elements</u>

- Your Name and Contact Information
- 1 Job Title
- A Summary
- Use of Strong, active Verbs
- Transferable Teaching Skills
- Measurable Results
- A Skills Section
- A Chronological list of Jobs from the past 10-12 years
- An Education Section
- Use of 10+ words from the Job Description to beat the ATS System
- 1-2 Pages (No more than two pages!)

One basic premise to follow when composing your resume is to stay away from lengthy descriptions, especially when describing past work experiences. It is a well-known fact that recruiters and HR professionals make decisions about a candidate within the *first 6-8 seconds* of viewing a resume. So, you must make an impact at the top of yours in the summary.

## The Job Title

The next section to include after your personal information is the Job Title (only one) you are applying for, i.e., Instructional Designer. Do not include a list of jobs as this can communicate a lack of focus in terms of what you are looking for. *Focusing on the job you are applying for* will help you concentrate on composing one resume at a time. Some people may argue this point, but it is essential to gear a resume to each specific job. You can have one foundational resume and add key words from job descriptions to create tailored resumes. In today's job market it is vital that you use such resumes. Today's resume must reflect not only your skills and experience but also your keen interest in the job and the organization.

## Summary

The next and most critical component is the summary. This is what recruiters *see first*. When you write this paragraph ask yourself these questions:

- What do I excel at?
- What sets me apart from others?
- What have I accomplished that has added value to my work/workplace or training?
- Which hard and soft skills can I highlight so hiring managers get a quick picture of what I can offer them?
- Which key words from the job description can I add that also reflect my skill set?

After you write the answers to these questions, compose a *brief* paragraph. Make sure to include action verbs.

Here are two examples of well-written summaries:

**Example 1: Mid to Senior Level Instructional Designer**

*Expert in Instructional Design, eLearning, and Corporate Training with over 20 years designing engaging learning experiences that enhance business performance and bring growth to diverse learners. I design and develop innovative and engaging eLearning courses, videos, infographics, job aids and more. I collaborate with all stakeholders, SMEs to establish effective ILT, blended learning, and eLearning requirements based on Adult Learning Theory (ADDIE). Expert in Needs Analysis, Front-end and Backward Design, Training Facilitation. Highest ROI using customized industry-based metrics and Kirkpatrick's Model for Evaluation.*

**Example 2: For Someone New to Instructional Design**

*Expert curriculum designer and customized learning designer. Adept at customized eLearning design and development, ILT and blended learning. Highly skilled at using ADDIE project management framework and Backward Design. Excellent writer of Outlines, Storyboards. Use industry-standard eLearning design, graphic design for all assets including Job Aides and Infographics. Compose engaging facilitator and participant guides aligned to learning goals of organization.*

After you write the summary, make sure you review it. It can take several revisions to get exactly what you want and need to communicate. I suggest combining language from the job description with some of the verbiage provided in Table 6.1.

When I compose my resume, I constantly go back to revise it by adding new skills and experiences to strengthen the language. My goal is to have a resume that shouts out my accomplishments and skills. I want you to do the same. It is helpful to get feedback on your resume as this will provide you with fresh insight. If you want expert advice, seek out a professional resume writer who has a good reputation. Make sure you ask for samples of their work first before hiring anyone. As always it is best to get a personal reference from a trusted source before hiring someone you do not know.

## Strong Verbs

A resume cannot show your true value to hiring managers without using strong language to get your message across. Using strong action verbs is vital in creating an outstanding resume. Here is sample text from a resume to give you an idea of how to add verbs. You want to write them at the very beginning of each bullet point.

- **Managed** Instructor-led training in research-based Writing program--achieved client satisfaction increasing learner academic achievement in writing skills by 40% across districts. Trained over 250 professionals.
- **Designed** and **delivered** professional development on-site, eLearning & blended learning for over 150 adult learners.
- **Managed** and increased sales by 25% of new education programs collaborating with stakeholders and sales team.
- **Spearheaded** client relations to determine key training needs (Needs Analysis) and determined optimal delivery methods with SMEs for highly effective professional development on-site, instructor-led, eLearning and blended learning.

When you review the language above, what do you notice? I used *spearheaded,* a synonym for the word *managed.* You will build a strong resume when you rely on synonyms. Using a Thesaurus is a helpful tool for this. While reading the information, did you recognize any language that represents the role of an ID? It is there. Once you start reading job ads you will be better able to begin writing using industry-related terminology. Table 6.1 is a brief list of strong verbs to add to your resume as you begin writing. Each column denotes a list of synonyms.

Table 6.1 List of Strong Verbs for Resumes

| create | manage | specialize | transform |
|---|---|---|---|
| originate | direct | commit | succeed |
| form | oversee | endeavor | overcome |
| begin | lead | deliver | accomplish |
| cause | head | undertake | win |
| produce | conduct | shape | commit |
| effect | spearhead | steer | improve |
| achieve | improve | partner | educate |
| boost | clarify | negotiate | consult |
| advance | customize | secure | recommend |
| decrease | modernize | forge | resolve |
| deliver | restructure | source | coach |

## Your Transferrable Teaching Skills- How to Communicate Them

Knowing what your skills are is one thing, being able to communicate them is another. As you go through this job change, take time to write down all your skills. It is easy to get them down on paper as you list each job, including volunteer work. I call this doing a "skills dump." List all your previous jobs then under each one, write down everything you accomplished. Did you write curriculum? Sponsor an after-school club? Sit on the leadership team? What were your responsibilities in each job or activity? Then, write down what you did and how these actions of yours affected change—change to your organization, students, school leaders, communities and more. Once you have this, the next step is to correlate these skills to the instructional designer role and eventually to a specific job description. Here are two examples, one for someone with business experience and one for educators:

<u>Example 1:</u>

I facilitated training for senior managers in a major bank. I organized the entire training, wrote the training handbook, communicated with all stakeholders about the event, created a slide deck explaining the new accounting methods for their budget process, and facilitated the training. Decreased overhead by 20% in keeping training in-house.

# Skills

Excellent communication skills     Writing          Accounting

PowerPoint               Training Facilitation      Training Handbook

## Instructional Design Language

- Created slide decks for ILT using PowerPoint.
- Facilitated training for senior management.
- Organized training implementation by contacting participants and organizing office space and technologies.
- Decreased overhead expenses by 20% maintaining internal training activity.
- Authored participant guides/workbooks customized to specific learners.

Example 2:

I sat on the school leadership team for expanding literacy skills through the MTSS/RTI system. With my leadership, 70 students' literacy scores increased by 30%. I wrote differentiated instructional materials and assessments for ESOL for English and U.S. History.

# Skills

Leadership                       Increased learning by 30%

English                            History

Author complex learning materials and assessments.

Manage student data- MTSS/RTI systems and upload them to school LMS.

## Instructional Design Language

- School leader who increased learner achievement by 30% in literacy skills.
- Authored customized learning materials and assessments for a diverse learner population of 70.
- Managed learner data on school based LMS.

When you write your resume, you must be able to take your school experience and translate it into the ID world and into the job description. This is how your resume will get noticed. In Table 6.2, I include more ID language--use this information as you begin composing. As you read and become familiar with ID job ads and descriptions you will be better able to transfer your skills directly onto your resume. My last piece of advice here is for you to write verbs in the past tense as you apply for new roles.

Table 6.2 Educator Skills Translated into Instructional Designer Skills

| Educator | Instructional Designer |
|---|---|
| Curriculum writer | ILT: Author slide decks, facilitator, and participant guides; design and develop eLearning content |
| Use of SmartBoard / ClearTouch board to teach lessons | Interactive, web-based learning/eLearning training development |
| Google Classroom/Blackboard | LMS Learning Management Systems |
| Differentiated Instruction and Assessment | Customized instruction / training |
| Teach students | Facilitate training for learners |
| Analyze student data from MTSS / RTI upload to school LMS | Upload learner data into LMS |
| Collaborate on Grade Teams/ PLCs and School Leadership teams, Literacy Coaches | Work collaboratively with SMEs |
| Teach a diverse body of students | Develop effective and engaging learning experiences for a diversified group of learners |
| Develop anchor charts and classroom resources | Design and develop infographics |
| Design handouts and worksheets to reinforce learning | Design and develop job aids and worksheets/workbooks customized to learners' needs |

## Measurable Results

How you affect growth in an organization and the ability to communicate is key in your landing an interview. Hiring managers expect to see how your work has affected positive change. So, show your savvy skills on your resume. In the two examples under Beating the ATS, notice how I cite measurable results. Using numbers and percentages is highly effective in showing growth. You can mention the number of learners affected by training, the percentage increase in areas of academic achievement, improved employee performance after training and more. Furthermore, using the skills dump mentioned earlier will aid you in describing your measurable achievements. Last, do not be shy about what you have accomplished! Let your resume scream success!

## Placing Skills on the Resume

You may not realize this, but everyone has soft skills and hard skills. Soft skills are those that are less technical, like excellent communication skills and analytical skills. Hard skills are those that show technical abilities, like knowledge of Articulate Storyline, Camtasia, MS Office, etc. When you list your soft skills, make sure they mirror the job description and the same goes for your technical skills. Recruiters look for this.

List your skills before or after the Experience section. I list mine after my work experience. Make sure to list your skills into two separate sections, Skills (for soft skills) and Technical Skills. Also, be certain to separate each skill. Using bullet points creates uniformity and readability. A resume requires white space. No one takes time to read a string of information.

## Work Experience

The work experience you list on your resume should highlight your skills and related experiences to the jobs you are applying for. Keep each concise and to the point. Use bullet points to promote readability. Do not use long sentences and avoid using "I." Under Resources I list a helpful book (that I have used) that includes dozens of effective resumes based on different jobs and industries. While you may have over 10 years' work experience, keep the job list to the past 10-12 years. Since I had a career in business prior to education, I keep a separate section that lists the companies and a few bullet points for my achievements that relate directly to the job descriptions. Because this experience is the oldest, I listed it at the end of all my other work experiences.

## Education

When you include your education, start with the last program you participated in and work backwards. The most current school should be on top. It is appropriate to add the years you studied and the year you graduated. List awards and honor societies. It is unnecessary to add the GPA. Listing Education at the bottom of the resume gives your experience and skills higher priority.

## Beating the ATS Computer System- Using the Right Words

For one job advertisement, companies and organizations can receive hundreds of applications. So, how do companies find the top candidates? By weeding out resumes that do not match the job description. The ATS (Applicant Tracking System) is a computer system used to read resumes and choose those with matching language, or key words, found in job descriptions. For you to get to the interview you must write a resume that mirrors the job description, in terms of using keywords for skills and work experience. Most experts recommend adding at least 10 words or phrases from the job ad to your resume so that the ATS picks up the resume. I know what you might be thinking: I worked so hard as a teacher, studied for months to become an instructional designer and this is still not enough? This is your *last big hurdle* to arrive at the interview. Your resume must reflect your interest in the job and the organization. It is as simple as that. While I mentioned that it is a clever idea to have one standard resume, you will need to build on it for each position you apply for. This process works. This tried and tested technique opens the way to the interview. It has opened doors for me. Here is an example of how to integrate verbiage from the job description into the work experience component of a resume.

Example Excerpt from an ID Job Description:

*This position is responsible for **designing, developing,** and maintaining curricula and programs used to train employees in a variety of functions. **Conducts needs assessments, selects instructional models, and designs instructional content.** **Reviews** and provides enhancements to instructional materials **in consultation with subject matter experts.***

Transferring ATS Language to Your Resume:

XYZ Company

Instructional Designer
- **Designed and developed** training programs for multiple functions.
- **Conducted Needs Assessments** for roll out of all trainings ensuring effective learning experiences for all 300 adult learners.
- **Selected instructional models** based on learner needs and consultation with **SMEs** and all stakeholders.
- **Designed all instructional content** for eLearning training and ILT learning experiences to broaden skills of 300 learners. Increased productivity by 25% over 6 months using internal metrics for ROI.
- **Reviewed all instructional materials,** job aids, facilitator, and participant guides in consultation with **SMEs** and all stakeholders.

Can you see how I recreated the job description into a resume example? One does not have to copy word for word, in fact it is best not to. What is best is to take the language used in a job ad and reword it in such a way that it reflects one's experience.

## The Resume – A Business Template

Now let us look at a standard resume. The template provided here (Figure 6.1) is meant to be a guide to show how to organize the information from your life into a resume. This template is business standard. My goal is to show you *how* to organize your information. On the template provided, text in the parentheses () is there as a reminder only. Do not include this information in your finished resume. Notice that I list both skills sections *before* the Education section to highlight these to hiring managers. After the Education section, the last section labeled Additional Information is where you can list your volunteer work, awards, publications, and memberships to professional organizations. Be sure to include hyperlinks under your name to include your LinkedIn profile and your portfolio. The portfolio is non-negotiable as well as your resume. You will need both to open doors to employment. Your resume should be 1-2 pages, not more than two pages. Ensure all tabs and margins are aligned to show uniformity and create readability Keep in mind that recruiters only give about 8 seconds to decide if you will make it to the next steps in the hiring process.

Using a fancy resume with colors and designs is appropriate for the on-site interview process. It is a clever idea to create one and print several copies for the meeting. Canva offers a lot of great templates for this as it is easy to create assorted designs within this top software. I encourage you *not* to use this when applying for jobs as the ATS system cannot read all the design elements and will delete the resume. There are many templates available online and in professional resume writing books for building effective resumes. I include two sources for this (under Resources).

Remember that a resume reflects your life experience, so be honest and only include what you have done and studied. Companies will check on your previous work experience by contacting them. Representatives typically call references and check on educational backgrounds as well. During my career in business, I had the responsibility of doing background checks. Sadly, I have seen new hires let go who misrepresented themselves on their resumes. Honesty is always the best policy.

A last tip for resume writing, summarize your information and keep it concise. Gear the language towards the organization and their needs by using the information provided in the job description. This is *the key* to getting you to the interview. After that, the rest is up to you.

## Figure 6.1 Resume Template

**Name**

City, state/country    cell phone    email address    LinkedIn link    website

---

### Instructional Designer (Job title)

(Summary: A brief paragraph that highlights your experience and skills that mirrors language in the job description. Make sure it is short in length.)

**Experience:** (Here is where you list your jobs in chronological order, with the newest first.)

XYZ Corporation, Houston, TX                              June 2020-Jan. 2023
Instructional Designer
- Managed large training project for 150 adult learners. Met project deadlines through collaboration with all stakeholders.
- Designed over 30 customized eLearning courses in Articulate Storyline, reducing skills and knowledge gaps for learners in 10 departments.
- Achieved increase in employee productivity by 35% using internal metrics.

ABC Company, New York, NY                              Jan. 2015-June 2020
Instructional Designer
- Spearheaded new training program for over 90 adult learners in Financial Advisory department resulting in increased productivity by 40% over 4 years.
- Developed new video technology integrated into eLearning platforms to improve learning experiences for over 200 learners.
- Managed training data on LMS, provided data to management for training program overhaul.

**Skills:** (Include verbiage from the job description and your experience.)

- Excellent Communication Skills
- Project Management
- Highly Analytical

**Technical Skills:** (Include technologies you know and are in the job ad.)

- Articulate 360: Rise & Storyline
- CANVA
- Camtasia
- Audacity, etc.

**Education:**

University of Virginia  Richmond, VA                    2019-2021
Master's, Instructional Design

**Additional Information:** (Add volunteer work, awards, publications, community service, professional organization memberships, etc.)

61

# Chapter 7 Job Hunting Tips that Pave Your Path

For you to land a job in Instructional Design, you need to conduct a proactive search. By this I mean you need to network, contact hiring managers, apply to jobs on a regular basis and reach out to professionals after the interview. One of the best ways of finding work is to network. Networking can be a mystery for many, especially for someone who has never worked in business before. Let me put you at ease—it is not difficult. It does, however, demand getting past any feelings of embarrassment or imposter syndrome by standing up for oneself. I say this because many educators have mentioned this in various online forums and directly to me. Remember when I said that educators are highly skilled, and better prepared to enter this profession? THAT'S YOU!

I realize that you have worked hard to become an educator and you are highly specialized and talented, but now you are starting over in unfamiliar territory. There is nothing shameful about this. I understand completely! Going into the unknown can shake you to your core. If you do not allow yourself to leap, you cannot grow! If you are feeling stuck, unmotivated, or anxious in any way, finding a teacher transition group can help you. I found a weekly teacher transition group on LinkedIn that has made all the difference. The support I received has been so great that I would not leave it for the world! You will find many groups on Facebook and in professional learning communities as well.

The priority in this chapter is to give you tips on networking, how to use internet job sites to find work and get volunteer clients. All these combined efforts will get you on the path towards your final goal-- an instructional design job. By putting yourself out there to as many audiences as possible, you will attract the attention you need, and you deserve. Because this is a multifaceted approach to job hunting, you need a daily plan of action. Keeping a calendar will help you write down daily goals and stick to them. I also suggest using a spreadsheet to keep track of your many applications, hiring managers and application status all in one place. I use MS Excel to help me stay organized but there are many other programs out there that will keep your information together. Choose one that will work for you, even a paper-based planner will get you going.

Networking

Networking involves contacting people outside your general circle on a regular basis. The easiest place to begin networking is within your own group of friends, fellow ID trainees and colleagues. Each one of your friends has family members who work. Every one of those people knows at least 20 other people—and so the network grows. Tap into the people you know first then let the group expand. This is the starting point of your network!

Of course, there are great ways to step up the expansion of your network by using the internet. Here is a list of networking groups to join:

- Facebook
  - Instructional Design Newbie
  - Articulate 360 Groups (Rise & Storyline)
  - Teachers in Transition
  - Transitioning Teachers
  - Instructional Designer
  - Instructional Design and eLearning Community: Upskilling and Job Transition
  - Instructional Design Jobs
  - Other Groups for Educators and Instructional Designers

- National Associations/Organizations
  - ATD (Association for Talent Development)
  - TLDC (The Training Learning & Development Conference)
  - Learning Guild

- LinkedIn
- Your ID Training Program Organization & Cohort
- Professional Memberships
- Universities and Colleges
- Local Commerce Department
- Local Networking Events

After looking at the list above, I hope you are thinking about organizations you belong to, have wanted to join, or know from friends, family, and colleagues. The main idea here is to join (if you have not already done so) and start talking to people. I have networked for years, so let me offer my own experience to give you some idea of how networking functions.

A while back I lived in New York City and would frequent various networking events. One night I found myself in a room with 500 people, yes that many! During the event, I connected at least 30 people to someone else. In fact, I even helped one person land a job in fashion design and I did not work in the fashion industry! Simply put, networking *is about making connections and helping others*. The techniques I used to "work the room" are not difficult to learn. It takes practice, so I recommend trying these out. These techniques will help you at both onsite and virtual meetings. First, I introduce myself by asking the other person about themselves. Show interest, *real* interest. Ask questions like, "What do you do for a living?" "If you could change your career, what would it be?" You can also ask them what they do for hobbies. Listen to what people say. You will find out about their interests and needs. Second, ask (yes ask) them how you could be of help to them. Then, tell them about yourself and what you are looking for—a job in instructional design. Make sure to add details like, "I finished training as an ID and would love to focus on eLearning course development. Do you know anyone who works in corporate training or Human Resources?" Next, ask the person for their business card or email address and follow up with them within the next 7-10 days. If you can provide them with assistance, do so. You will be rewarded in the end. If the person cannot help you, ask them for a contact of theirs who might be able to and get their information as well.

This is how networking operates—offering help and receiving information. It is a *two-way* street. If you are at an in-person event, make sure to give every person a firm handshake and make good eye contact. Wear your name tag (one usually gets one) on the right-hand side of your outfit because most people look on the right-hand side when shaking hands. This makes your name memorable. (So does adding a hobby or an interesting fact about yourself under your name, like "accountant and violinist.") It is also important to wear professional clothing—a pants suit with a blazer or whatever makes you comfortable if it is polished. If you attend an event with business professionals, you will want to wear a blazer or jacket. Wearing a colorful blouse or shirt underneath also helps people remember you. Last, remember to thank everyone you meet, especially those who offer you contacts or other information. This is how to network. On the internet, follow the same steps and be sure to show your appreciation for others. You are inviting a new group of professionals into your life, so make a good impression. Be sincere and be yourself!

When you are contacting professionals online, it is vital that your first contact is one in which you show interest in their career and organization. It is especially important to do this. Why? There are two reasons. One, you want to show that you have done your homework about the person and the organization. This communicates authentic interest. Two, without this authenticity there is no obligation on the side of the person you contacted to reciprocate. In other words, coming out and declaring you need a job as the first communication will do nothing but turn the person away. Put yourself in their shoes. Would you want others to contact you without regard to who you are or where you work? As I stated earlier, sincerity is key in creating and maintaining a network.

## Looking for Work on the Web

Using the internet to scope out work is a process, another crucial step along your career path. So, begin with jobsites that have opened doors for people in your network then branch out to new sites. My advice is to use as many job sites as possible, without overburdening yourself. The more websites you are actively using and register with the more visibility you will have.

Job sites offer jobseekers multiple ways to find a job. Creating an account on these sites will help you focus your search and get you noticed. First, you set up search engines to locate instructional design jobs and related job titles (eLearning designer, L& D design, etc.) by creating a job search with notifications. Second, choose the option of allowing recruiters to view your uploaded resume. Make sure to expand your visibility by choosing jobs in multiple geographic locations or nationwide. The more flexible you are with relocating, the better chances your application has of moving forward. Third, most search engines will send you regular email notifications of jobs based on your job search specifications. This way, you will have timely access to jobs as they become available. If you can apply to jobs as soon as they come up, the sooner your resume will get considered. It is a huge advantage to apply early before the hiring authority becomes inundated with applications.

Instructional design jobs are listed under various job titles. So, when you do a job search try these similar job titles in the search engine listed on the next page.

## Alternate Titles Used to Find Instructional Designer Roles

- o  Instructional Designer
- o  eLearning Designer/Developer
- o  eLearning Specialist
- o  L&D Designer
- o  Blended Learning Lead
- o  ILT Developer
- o  Training Lead
- o  Training Facilitator (training lead)
- o  Learning Designer
- o  Learning Developer
- o  Corporate Learning & Development Specialist
- o  Manager, Training
- o  Technical Course Developer
- o  Articulate Storyline Designer/Developer
- o  Articulate Rise Designer/Developer
- o  Adobe Captivate Developer

## LinkedIn

Using LinkedIn is a powerful networking tool when used effectively. Like many online resources, there is a way to use LinkedIn to maximize your impact. This platform is unique as it allows members to build a large network filled with people to connect with. Here are a few tips to get you started connecting. First, create a LinkedIn profile at www.linkedin.com The platform will guide you as you fill out your experience, education and more. Once your profile is complete, you will choose privacy settings. Choosing "Everyone" on LinkedIn will allow more professionals access to you and your posts.

The first thing in setting up your profile after your name is to upload your photograph, making sure it is one that is friendly and business like. Then, add the job title, or titles you have. Notice in the screenshot below that I have three titles. You do not want to add too many as recruiters use this information to screen candidates. Over time it is appropriate to update your titles. Here is my LinkedIn example:

# Erika L. Martin (She/Her)
## Instructional Designer | Teacher Advocate | Author

Under this section you will see the following hashtags. You add these under Resources, Creator Mode. Here is where you go to turn on the option that allows others to follow your posts based on your areas of interest. (You can choose only five.) Hashtags are important as they attract other professionals to your posts. Also, there are interest groups on LinkedIn based on hashtags that you can join. Using hashtags is another opportunity to meet other members and expand your network. Here are mine:

| | |
|---|---|
| #instructionaldesign | #learninganddevelopment |
| #transitioningteachers | #elearningdesign |

Below these is an Open to work box. This is an important part of the profile—it is where you add pertinent information for recruiters. Here you indicate five job titles, workplaces (onsite and remote), job locations (up to 5), start date and job types. At the bottom of this section, you can choose to show you are Open for Work which lets all recruiters and all members of LinkedIn know. Or you can choose Recruiters Only. These recruiters pay fees to LinkedIn to get access to professionals. This is a smaller pool of recruiters, so it is to your advantage to put up the green sign, Open for Work.

> Open to work
> Learning And Development Specialist, Education...
> See all details

[Images: www.linkedin.com]

After you have finished completing the top portion of your profile, the next is the About section. Here is where you offer recruiters and other members an outstanding picture of your career. I do not recommend putting your resume here. This space is meant for career highlights instead. At the beginning of my About section, I added a summary statement about myself. This should be a strong statement that is eye catching. Below this I divided information into three categories: What I am All About, How I Bring Value to the Workplace, and What Made Me Who I am Today. After this information I list my skills and a motto. These are my suggestions. In this section avoid writing long paragraphs. Instead divide your information up so it becomes more readable.

About    ✎

During my successful careers in business and education, I have affected high growth. I have created effective & visually appealing training programs for international corporations, global organizations, school districts and more. With years of experience designing training and a natural talent for design, I create courses based on adult learning theory. My courses meet the needs of organizations that lift their employees to higher ground.

The rest of the profile is self-explanatory, but I do want to mention the Skills section. Here you can list dozens of skills and have others endorse you for these skills. Once you gain new skills, ask others to endorse you. (There is a button for this.) This will make your profile stand out. Make sure to keep the top three skills relevant to your new career. You will also need to keep this section current.

Skills        ( Demonstrate skills ) ✎

🅱 You've added the maximum number of skills

Interview Preparation

▨ Corporate Trainer/Marketing Specialist at Private Industry

Once your profile is complete, connect with your network and begin to expand it. Be sure to include new contacts you have made. You might include people you have met during your instructional design course. Then, start searching for professionals in the field of instructional design. Here is an effortless way to find teachers already working in instructional design.

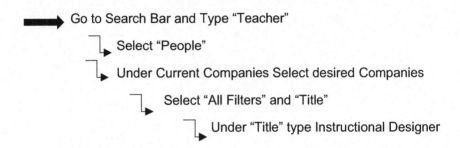

Go to Search Bar and Type "Teacher"

Select "People"

Under Current Companies Select desired Companies

Select "All Filters" and "Title"

Under "Title" type Instructional Designer

When you follow the steps above, you will get a list of teachers who are now instructional designers within a specific company/organization. You can use these same steps to search for any professional within specific companies. This is a great segway into growing your network, so try it out!

There is another section worth mentioning called Featured. Here you can upload your newly designed assets, client projects, websites and more. I have a link to my website here as well as my publication. This section is prime real estate for highlighting your best work, so use it wisely!

**Featured**

Link

Erika Martin

Instructional Designer

CANVA/www.linked.com]

When contacting other LinkedIn members, remember to follow the basic networking protocols I mentioned. Ask insightful questions before explaining you are looking for work. If you have a LinkedIn Premium account, you will have access to professionals who are 2nd and 3rd in your LinkedIn network through premium mail called InMail. LinkedIn Premium is not free, after the initial 30-day trial it is $39.99 per month for the basic Career Plan.

LinkedIn has algorithms that help increase the visibility of its members. These can only work to your advantage if you are using LinkedIn on a regular basis. Here is a list of tips that to help get you noticed:

- Create 2-3 Posts a week.
- Like 3-5 Posts or Add Comments to others' Posts 3 times/week at minimum, 3 times/daily is recommended.
- Send 2 Connection Requests stating why you would like to connect.

LinkedIn Tips (cont.)

- Join LinkedIn networking groups.
- List your Skills and request Endorsements.
- Under Features add Designs/other Assets.
- Upload Your Resume or Add a Resume Link.
- Add a Link to your Website under Profile and Features.
- Under Creator Mode add 5 Hashtags # to display your interests.

Other Job Sites

There are many job search sites online, so knowing which ones will help you as you begin to look for instructional design jobs is key. Whichever ones you choose, create an account where you can upload or write your resume directly there. As with LinkedIn, instructional design jobs are listed under various titles. Start with the titles I listed earlier in the chapter.

One of the top job sites is ZipRecruiter. There is a great advantage to using ZipRecruiter as it hosts the largest number of jobs on job boards, over one million. Many job seekers, including myself, have found this website user friendly. I also recommend putting your resume on Indeed. I have had success finding work using their website. Keep in mind that these job sites are for searching jobs; they are not networking platforms. Below is a list of the most popular job search sites.

- ZipRecruiter www.ziprecruiter.com (Over 1M jobs)
- Indeed www.indeed.com
- Monster www.monster.com
- Glassdoor www.glassdoor.com provides salary information
- Ladders www.theladders.com for jobs that pay $100K+

## General Career Information

There are many career seekers looking for distinct roles or who would like more information on where they can use their talents. This book is meant to support educators in navigating the instructional design career. Yet, there is an excellent handbook from the U.S. Bureau of Labor Statistics that can guide you in a general career search. This book, the *Occupational Outlook Handbook,* is a compilation of hundreds of job titles and job descriptions. It includes market data, potential growth for specific jobs, salary expectations and more. Under Resources you will find the website to access this valuable resource. I used this guide when I was in college, and it helped me make informed decisions about connecting my values, interests, and skills to the right fitting career. You will find it most helpful. You will find Instructional Design under Training.

## Get a Volunteer Client

As you may know already, the workplace is a competitive one and at times, highly competitive. A way to get an advantage over other candidates is to gain experience with a Volunteer Client. This could be a non-profit or for-profit organization. Many ID training programs include this experience as you study. If, however, they do not, it will help your career by working voluntarily on a short-term project. Why? You will grow professionally by using your skills as you complete projects. During the ID job interview process, you will be able to share your volunteer experience and how you made a difference. This is important for passing the interview. I know many transitioned teachers who got their full-time jobs because they had done volunteer work before. You may know the adage: Experience before everything. Well, it rings true for instructional designers even more so. The reason is that we work in a technical field which demands the ability to demonstrate technical skills relating to real-world problems. In short, if you can help solve a training issue you will be highly valuable to any employer.

Finding a Volunteer Client is not difficult or complex. However, you will need to be proactive in your search and continuously contact professionals on a regular basis. After you apply, you will go through an interview process. During the interview, you will be asked about your website and your portfolio. Trust me, I have gone through this process. The very first questions hiring managers asked me involved gaining access to my website (portfolio), my interest in the company and even having me evaluate their online information. So, have your website up and running as soon as possible with some of your best work presented there. I cannot stress this enough! You cannot compete with hundreds of others without proof of your talent in instructional design and development. Finally, do your homework and learn about the organizations and the projects you could potentially work on. Showing keen interest is vital to any employer.

Here is a list of Volunteer Organizations that offer volunteer and freelancing work opportunities. Again, this is a brief list to get you started.

Volunteer Work Websites

- www.volunteermatch.org
- www.fiverr.com freelancing
- www.upwork.com freelancing
- www.catchafire.org
- www.designxhumanity.com

## Additional Support

Looking for work is challenging, and no person should endeavor this entirely on their own. Having support is not only helpful, but essential. Earlier, I mentioned a Teacher Transition support group on LinkedIn. As you begin to look for work, you will find other teachers looking to change careers. Many of them are on Facebook and LinkedIn, so I suggest starting there. Use the list at the beginning of this chapter. I am in most of these groups and can attest to the fact that the educators and other professionals there are most helpful.

Recently, I have met some educators who for no fault of their own found themselves isolated and demotivated as their job searches lingered on. The longer it takes you to land a job, the more stamina you will need to keep going. So, join a group of like-minded professionals who are experiencing similar challenges. Another great resource is a career coach. They help clients focus on goal setting while making concrete plans for growth. You can find these wonderfully helpful professionals on LinkedIn as well.

Your career path depends on the steps you take and follow until you reach your goal. The tips I provide here are those I followed myself which enabled me to reach my destination—becoming an instructional designer. You will be successful; believe in yourself and know you are not alone. Joining other teachers on your way will give you encouragement. Who knows, you might make friends while expanding your network and even help another teacher find their job. Giving to others as you go along your path shall force the universe to give back to you!

Finally, the best way to look for work is to let others know that you are looking for it. Present yourself in the best way possible. Do the groundwork and trust in the process. Your success is determined by your willingness to persevere. Remember, do not underestimate the impact of networking or volunteering. Both will lead you to meet other professionals who may lead you to your dream job. All of this takes time. You can do this! Rely on your own support system and network to boost you forward. The next step in this book is to give you time for introspection—a necessary step for creating change. You are embarking on a whole new work life. To help facilitate this major change allow yourself the freedom to think about it first.

# Chapter 8 Reflection Leads to Better Decision-Making

When I was considering transitioning into instructional design, I was not sure this was the right career for me. So, after reading about it and connecting with other instructional designers I grabbed my journal and began writing down what I wanted out of my next career. I chose to take the time to do the reflection that would give me greater clarity about what I wanted from my work and my life. In the end, this process also became the path for setting my personal goals, goals that got me moving in the right direction. Having done a great deal of my own introspection, I believe it to be a necessary (and highly effective) part of creating change in one's life. You are about to embark on a new career, an entirely different work life. This is a major life change. You cannot embrace change unless you ask yourself *what you want and how you are going to get there.* You have heard it a hundred times: Planning is key to success—and it is! But to get to your plan, you must first have a serious conversation with yourself. In short, you must decide first what it is you WANT. If you do not know the answer to that question, you could waste precious time pursuing goals that do not match your values, needs or interests.

In support of your journey, I have compiled a list of questions. I suggest copying these questions into a journal or notebook, write your answers, revisit them, and see over time if your answers change. They will, and that is normal. It is a sign of personal growth. Feel free to add your own questions, comments, and concerns during this important process. The important thing is to write your thoughts down so you can gain clarity of mind and purpose. Reflection opens the door to change as one looks at past experiences and gains wisdom into what worked and what did not. What was once a fulfilling career has lost its luster, why? Only you can answer that question. Reflection allows one to make better decisions. If a former job no longer fits your needs, then what does? You will find the answers to these questions when you give yourself the time and opportunity to do self-reflection. The answers are waiting, they are inside of you. Take time to listen.

So, here are the questions I developed and worked on in my own journal. These questions challenged my thinking and eventually led me to change my career. The focus here is on the now; learn from the past and move forward. It will also help you to keep your mind on positives, rather than negatives. I know the daily challenges and stress involved in teaching; I lived it. Do not allow this to cloud your emotions, thoughts, or your decisions. Remember, you have the power within yourself to make the changes you need and the will to build this new life you want. If I can do it, so can you! (Not to mention the thousands of other educators who have already transitioned.)

## Self-Reflection Questions

What aspects of teaching (or my current role in education) do I enjoy the most?

Which teaching skills do I excel at? Write a list of these. This will help you realize how skilled you are.

Look at your skills list above. Choose 3-5 top skills. Do any of these skills have anything to do with curriculum design, course design or visual design?

What has not worked for me in my last career? Why not? What has worked for me?

What excites me about a career in instructional design?

Which components of ID interests me the most?

Will designing learning experiences for adults fulfill me? Why or why not?

What are some things I have designed in my education career that correlate to graphic design? Have I found working with colors and graphics rewarding/interesting?

What kind of plan can I put into place for 2023 that will lead me to transition into an ID role?

What challenges do I foresee in the next months that could potentially slow my plan down? How will I meet these challenges?

What do I want to accomplish towards my goal in becoming an ID within the next month, next three months, next six months, within the next year? How will I take the first step(s)?

Which aspects of working in education do I *not* want in my next career? (Try not to go overboard!)

My goal for you throughout this reflective process is to really think about your past work, how it relates to instructional design and how you can begin thinking about making a real plan to become an instructional designer. As I mentioned, revisiting these questions more than once will help you solidify your reasoning for selecting this career or help you change your mind to choose another path for your life. (That is ok too!)

Keep in mind that this process is just for you. However, if you want to share your thoughts with a significant other, do so. It is often empowering to have someone else be a sounding board, someone who supports you through this important process of personal growth and change.

The next step to moving you onto your path as an instructional designer is to make the plan that will push you forward into your new role and new life!

# Chapter 9 A Career Transition Plan to Propel You Forward

So, now that you have taken the necessary time to make the decision to go forward, the next step is to make a concrete plan to get you into your new ID career. Even before you plan it is essential to look at challenges that are part of creating change. The most common ones are the time commitment, the financial investment, and the right training program.

Before I left my teaching job, I had already researched various training programs and mapped out what I needed in terms of finances and time. I highly suggest you do the same. It can be a trap to give into frustration or any other emotions you might be feeling now while you are still in education. This is normal. Just do not let your emotions make the decisions for you! Instead, sit down on a calm afternoon or evening to map out your challenges. Make sure you are realistic about your current situation and consider any constraints you might have now or those that could arise later. This could be as simple as finishing the school year, teaching summer school, raising children and so on. Address your challenges first so that you can move forward to creating your plan. So, let us begin with that list first. Just like you did with the questions before, it will help you to copy this into a notebook or journal to fill it out. To get you started I have added some of the typical challenges any career change can present.

**Financial Commitment**- Consider how you will cover the added expense of studying to become an instructional designer. I found it helpful and practical to have saved the necessary money before I studied. Make and commit to a budget for this and decide how long you might need to save, which may determine when you begin your training. For this conversation, you may want to consult your spouse or significant other, as these decisions will affect them as well.

**Time Commitment** – Studying requires time. Based on your current situation, what amount of time can you realistically give to the planned program of study? If it is for 6 months, 3 hours a day, how will you meet this requirement? Write down a realistic time slot that covers your studies. It is as simple as "I can dedicate _____ hours a day/week. Make sure to stick to this commitment! Training can move quickly, or it can be self-paced. Depending on your timetable of when you plan to study, you will need to stick to this goal.

**Coursework** - The type of program or coursework you choose will determine the time and money investments. Ask yourself: What type of training program can I realistically do over the next _____ weeks/months/year? Get a calendar and map out the training. This will help you keep to all the deadlines and meet your training/educational goals.

**Additional Resources** – No training program covers everything. In fact, it is quite common to purchase software licenses and books as part of your training to prepare for this new career. You may also wish to take extra courses through various organizations in addition to your main training program. Make a list of these and the added costs so that you will not have surprises down the road. Feel free to use Table 9.1 to organize your own information.

Table 9.1 My Training Plan & Challenges

| Challenges | My Plan |
|---|---|
| Ex. Financial Commitment | I will save $3000 over the next 6 months to pay for my training program by _____. |
| Time | |
| Coursework | |
| Additional Resources | |
| | |
| | |
| | |
| | |
| | |

Now that you know your challenges, you are ready to make your annual plan. Use the template on the next page. I also include a daily planner to help keep you organized. Feel free to print all three planners for easy use.

Happy planning!

# MY CAREER PLAN

MY NEEDS/VALUES

MY INTERESTS/SKILLS

MY CHALLENGES

WHAT I WANT NOW / HOW TO GET THERE

# DAILY PLANNER

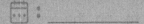 : _____

S M T W T F S

## TODAY'S GOAL

## TASKS

1.

2.

3.

## ME TIME

## CONTACTS/JOB SITES

## Last Things to Consider Before Traveling Your New Path

Change is good. It fosters growth—both professional and personal. However, before diving into any new career there are a few prudent things to consider. Leaving one profession to begin another requires a financial buffer to cover life's expenses. So, it is a clever idea to work until you can make a smooth transition. For example, taking ID coursework at night, on the weekends and during the summer until you are ready to work as an ID will reduce financial strain. Many transitioned teachers make a 6-month to 12-month plan before they begin their studies. I did. My 6-month plan made all the difference. I highly encourage you to do the same. The better the plan the more likely your efforts will be rewarded. Use the plan template provided here or use one you like. The main thing is to put all your ducks in place before you set out on your ID career path. My wish for you is to have the smoothest ride possible, so plan as far ahead as you are able.

As you embark into a whole new profession, be kind to yourself and be patient. You will be treading new waters here, so give yourself the time to learn, practice, and grow. There are various aspects to instructional design-- choose one that interests you and become good at it. Remember there are many others out there learning alongside you. Reach out to that larger community of learners for growth and support.

In conclusion, I hope the information provided here will get you well on your way! I can honestly say that this role has offered me the analytical, design, instructional, and writing aspects of work that I love. Now that you have discovered more about this exciting career, I hope you are ready to step out onto your new path. As you pursue it, I wish you enormous success! Just know I am rooting for you from here!

# Resources

Publications:

Boller, S., & Fletcher, R., 2020. *Design thinking for training and development*. Association for Talent Development.

Malamed, C., 2015. *Visual design solutions*. Wiley.

Moore, C., 2017. *Map It: The hands-on guide to strategic training design*. Montesa Press.

Slade, T., 2020. *The eLearning designer's handbook: A practical guide to the eLearning development process for new eLearning designers.* (2nd Ed.) Independently Published.

Yate, M., 2015. *Knock 'em dead cover letters*. (11th Ed.) Jumpingdude Media.

Yate, M., 2016. *Knock 'em dead resumes*. (12th Ed.) Adams Media.

Additional Resources/Websites:

ATD www.td.org

Cara North, ID Community Supporter  Cara North | LinkedIn

David Kelly, CEO, The Learning Guild David Kelly | LinkedIn

Melissa Milloway, This Side Up Newsletter LinkedIn (2) Melissa Milloway | LinkedIn

The Learning Guild www.learningguild.com

NovoEd  NovoEd: Online Learning Platform | Collaborative Learning for the Enterprise

The Training, Learning and Development Community & Conference www.TheTLDC.com

U.S. Bureau of Labor Statistics- Occupational Outlook Handbook www.bls.gov

Federal Jobs Site  www.usajobs.gov

# Resources

## Resume Writing:

www.resumegenius.com

https://www.themuse.com/advice/185-powerful-verbs-that-will-make-your-resume-awesome

## Expert in LinkedIn, Resume Writer:

Jessica Hernandez, CPBS, CDCS | LinkedIn

https://www.resume-now.com/job-resources/resumes

https://www.colorado.edu/career/job-searching/resumes-and-cover-letters/resumes/action-verbs-use-your-resume

https://www.myperfectresume.com/

# References

Morrison, G.R., Ross, S.J., Morrison, J.R. and Kalman, H.K., 2019. *Designing effective instruction*. John Wiley & Sons.

Piskurich, G.M., 2015. *Rapid instructional design: Learning ID fast and right*. John Wiley & Sons.

## Websites:

Andragogy - Wikipedia

File: ADDIE Model of Design.jpg - Wikipedia

www.bls.gov

www.canva.com

www.freepik.com

www.resumegenius.com

https://www.usnews.com/education/online-education/education/online-instructional-media-design-rankings

## About the Author

Erika L. Martin worked in international business as a corporate trainer for over a decade before becoming an educator. For 15 years, she has led significant changes in education as an educator, teacher-trainer, mentor, coach, and education consultant. Her training focuses on improving pedagogy for English Learners and Writing Across the Curriculum K-8. As an instructional designer she thrives on eLearning design and development and visual design. In her free time, she enjoys family and her two Corgis, Buddy, and Rudy. Her passions include art history, French cooking, handbag design, traveling, and growing roses.

Please Stay Connected & Share Your Thoughts on the Book!

Email Book Comments to: empowerededucators@aol.com

LinkedIn: Erika L. Martin | LinkedIn